Endeavour

Encounters, stories and objects of the ship that changed the world

AUSTRALIAN NATIONAL
MARITIME MUSEUM

Published by
The Australian National Maritime Museum
2 Murray Street Sydney NSW 2000
Australia
www.sea.museum

© The Australian National Maritime Museum 2023
First published 2023

10 9 8 7 6 5 4 3 2 1

The Australian National Maritime Museum is a statutory authority of the Australian Government.

 A catalogue record for this book is available from the National Library of Australia

ISBN 978-1-761-45077-8

Commissioning editor Peter Fray
Project manager and editor Janine Flew
Designer James de Vries
Printers Ellikon Fine Printers (Australia); Leo Paper Group (China)

The Australian National Maritime Museum acknowledges the Gadigal people of the Eora nation as the traditional custodians of the bamal (earth) and badu (waters) on which the museum is located. We also acknowledge all traditional custodians of the land and waters throughout Australia and pay our respects to them and their cultures, and to elders past and present. Members of Aboriginal and Torres Strait Islander communities are advised that some of the people mentioned in writing or depicted in illustrations in this book have passed away.

Become a member of the Australian National Maritime Museum. See our website www.sea.museum

Front cover The *Endeavour* replica at sea. Image ANMM
Inside front cover Original hull plan of HMB *Endeavour*, dated 25 April 1768. Australasian Pioneers' Club collection

Contents

The ship that changed

by Daryl Karp AM

Director, Australian National Maritime Museum

HIS MAJESTY'S Bark *Endeavour* is one of history's most significant vessels — on a global scale. Where this small ship travelled and the events that it took part in were fundamental to shaping our world today.

By telling and retelling its story through different eyes, *Endeavour* can also become a doorway to understanding the world we want to shape for tomorrow.

Endeavour played a pivotal, and contested, role in the narratives of several nations — not least Australia. It is a vessel from the Age of Enlightenment, the time of an outpouring of scientific, political and philosophical knowledge from western Europe in the 17th and 18th centuries.

Between 1768 and 1771, under the command of Lieutenant James Cook, *Endeavour* sailed to the South Pacific, first to witness the transit of Venus, an important moment in the annals of science and navigation, and then to harvest the natural bounty of many nations. But it also carried with it secret orders: to discover and claim the fabled Great South Land in the name of Britain's King George III.

Two years into the voyage, on 29 April 1770, *Endeavour* arrived on the east coast of Australia, in a place Cook named Botany Bay — known as Kamay to its Indigenous inhabitants, the Gweagal and Gamayngal clans of the Dharawal nation.

Cook and his crew could not have foreseen that this moment would become a symbol of European colonisation, nor that they and their ship would leave enduring legacies — many of them negative — for First Nations peoples around the Pacific.

Eight years later, *Endeavour* (by then renamed *Lord Sandwich*) ended its voyaging by playing a small role in the birth of the United States as a sovereign nation.

Maritime archaeologists from the Australian National Maritime Museum confirmed in 2022 that a shipwreck site in Newport Harbor, Rhode Island, contained the remains of *Endeavour*. It had been scuttled there by the British in 1778 to stall the advancing French navy, which had joined the American side in the Revolutionary War (1775–83).

Endeavour — the former coal-carrier that had sailed the world in the spirit of discovery — ended its days as a sunken prison ship on the losing side of a war that precipitated the transportation of British convicts to Australia. A decade later, the First Fleet of convicts arrived in Sydney Cove (Warrane).

Endeavour's final resting place has, like so much in its life, sparked debate and controversy. This modest ship has left scientific, cultural and political legacies that span Europe, North and South America, Polynesia, Aotearoa New Zealand and Australia.

It has been the subject of 174 books in the past six decades — including ten books or reports published by the Australian National Maritime Museum — mostly about the ship, Cook and Joseph Banks, the wealthy English botanist who paid £10,000 to secure places for himself and his entourage on the vessel.

So, why produce a new book? Why not simply republish one of the many others?

History is neither static nor one-dimensional. *Endeavour* is always open to reinterpretation. Its story is a living one, which is represented at the Australian National Maritime Museum, the home since 2005 of the only replica of Cook's *Endeavour*.

In 2020, in what was the 250th anniversary of *Endeavour*'s arrival in Kamay, many opportunities for truth-telling were dulled, or even silenced, due to the COVID-19 pandemic.

Voices from the Aboriginal and Torres Strait Islander descendants living along the eastern coast of Australia were denied the opportunity to be heard. Fortunately, artworks and interviews by visual artists and community representatives who chose to tell their stories are represented in the collections of the museum. Some are included in this book.

the world

Endeavour is always open to reinterpretation, and its story is a living one

The construction of the *Endeavour* replica is a remarkable story and worthy of retelling.
Between 1988 and 1994, in Fremantle, Western Australia, a determined and dedicated team of craftspeople, boatbuilders, philanthropists and historians re-created the vessel in such detail that the word 'replica' hardly does the ship justice.

A great achievement in itself, the replica also played a significant role in the discovery of the original *Endeavour*'s wreck off Rhode Island, USA.

The differences between the replica and the original are due to location: boatbuilders in northern England and Fremantle, respectively, used locally sourced wood and other materials. But the techniques used to construct the replica mirrored those of the original to such an exact extent that when it came to identifying the wreck off Rhode Island, the 'new' *Endeavour* proved an invaluable resource.

Maritime archaeologists surveying what was believed to be the HMB *Endeavour* wreck compared, for instance, the timber joinery used in making the replica to identify the same joinery on the wreck (see page 48). Having the replica made identifying the wreck quicker, easier and more accurate. The contemporary ship had, in effect, reached back to lend a helping hand to history.

The *Endeavour* replica is a working vessel. It has undertaken many extraordinary voyages, to virtually all parts of the globe. The replica has lasted more than twice as long as the original and continues to provide visitors — and sailors — with the physical sense of what it was like to live and work aboard an 18th-century ship.

This book, then, represents the next chapter in *Endeavour*'s story.

We have chosen to tell part of the story via objects linked to *Endeavour*. Most are held by the Australian National Maritime Museum. We have drawn on the museum's vast reservoir of expertise and thank the many writers, from within the museum and outside, who have contributed to this book.

We have also drawn on other objects that inform contemporary and historical views of *Endeavour*. These artefacts have helped us revisit key moments in the story of the ship, its people and its legacy — and to honour the extraordinary work in the discovery and identification of the wreck off Rhode Island and in building the replica in Western Australia.

This will not be the final story of the impact of *Endeavour*, and certainly not the only place to discuss its role in the history of colonisation and dispossession of First Nations and the ongoing impact of European settlement on Indigenous peoples and cultures — but, as historian Maria Nugent writes in her book *Captain Cook Was Here*, a detailed account of the eight days and nights that Cook and company spent at the place he initially called Stingray Bay before settling on Botany Bay:

> *When it comes to the matter of Captain Cook in Australia as well as in Australian history and imagination, one might say that it's a classic case of always beginning, never ending. This is a story still in the process of being told, a history that is constantly in the making. There is always something new, or more, to say.*

The Australian National Maritime Museum seeks to explore all narratives from multiple points of view. Truth-telling is an essential part of our mission.

Endeavour is a human achievement. In its time, its voyage from Britain to South America, Tahiti, Aotearoa New Zealand and Australia was the equivalent of landing on the moon. Its discovery in Rhode Island, too, is a feat of great skill and persistence, as was the making of the replica more than 30 years ago.

Tens of thousands of people visit the *Endeavour* replica at its mooring at the Australian National Maritime Museum every year, and the museum does all it can to ensure visitors see the ship and its historical significance in many ways.

We hope this book contributes to that.

The many lives of HMB *Endeavou*

THE SHIP that James Cook commanded on his first voyage to the Pacific would have attracted little attention in any English port in the 18th century, being typical of the rather unglamorous ships employed in the coal trade. Hundreds of colliers plied England's east coast between London and Newcastle, where their flat-bottomed design was ideal for working the tidal River Tyne and laying alongside to load coal.

Built in Whitby in 1764 and launched as *Earl of Pembroke*, the ship was originally fitted with cabins and storerooms under the fore and quarterdecks, with an enormous cargo space (hold) in the rest of the hull. When, in 1768, the Royal Society lobbied the Admiralty to send an expedition to the island of Tahiti to observe the transit of Venus, the commissioners of the navy suggested that a converted collier would serve to carry the large number of men, equipment and stores needed for such a voyage. The Admiralty agreed, and after a thorough survey, *Earl of Pembroke*

was accepted and commissioned as His Majesty's Bark (HMB) *Endeavour*.

Endeavour proved an inspired choice, arriving in Tahiti in good time to observe the transit of Venus (see page 14) before continuing west and charting first New Zealand then Australia's east coast, where its flat bottom was critical in saving the expedition after the ship ran aground on the Great Barrier Reef. The crew were able to refloat the badly damaged ship but, with the pumps barely able to keep it afloat, they were extremely lucky to find a place on the nearby coast where *Endeavour* was repaired in a protected river — now named Endeavour River. Permanent repairs were made when the ship reached Batavia (now Jakarta) and the expedition returned safely to England in July 1771. Almost immediately, it was tasked with a new service.

Since 1765, England had laid claim to the Falkland Islands, in the South Atlantic Ocean, and established

LEFT *The Bark*, Earl of Pembroke, *later* Endeavour, *leaving Whitby Harbour in 1768*, Thomas Luny, c 1790. National Library of Australia nla.obj-134301494

ABOVE Engraving of Captain James Cook after a 1776 painting by Nathaniel Dance. ANMM Collection 00000373

Why choose Cook?

James Cook (born 1728) was 40 years old at the start of the *Endeavour* voyage. Born in Yorkshire, the son of a farm labourer, Cook had gone to sea at the age of 18 as an apprentice in the trade that carried coal between London and towns on the east coast of England. He learnt quickly and, after further experience sailing in the Baltic trade, he was offered command of a ship, but chose instead to join the Royal Navy in 1755. Initially rated able seaman, within a month he was promoted to master's mate, serving two years on *HMS Eagle* in the English Channel.

When hostilities between Britain and France broke out in 1757, Cook was promoted again — this time as master of the new 60-gun *HMS Pembroke*, crossing the Atlantic to North America. As master, Cook was responsible for all aspects of navigating the ship and occupied an important position within the ship's hierarchy — second only to the captain and first lieutenant. In Canada, Cook found a mentor in army engineer Samuel Holland, who opened his eyes to the most advanced surveying procedures.

Following the defeat of France, Cook took part in the survey of Newfoundland and Nova Scotia, and in 1764 was given command of *HMS Grenville* to carry on the work. His fine surveys over the next three years brought him to the attention of the Admiralty and were later published. During this period, Cook also sent a paper to the Royal Society describing a solar eclipse he had witnessed. As a result of these achievements, when the decision was made to send a ship to Tahiti, Cook was well placed to be given command of the expedition.

Now commissioned lieutenant, Cook's command of the *Endeavour* voyage provided ample proof of his skills. He charted new lands, observed the transit of Venus, maintained the health of his crew and overcame the stranding on Endeavour Reef. He also successfully negotiated the social differences between himself, Joseph Banks and other supernumeraries brought aboard for the voyage.

Once back in England, the voyage's botanists, Banks and Daniel Solander, received most of the public applause, but for those who understood the rigours of such a voyage, it was Cook who deserved the real praise. He was promoted to commander in 1772 and soon given command of a second voyage of exploration. By the time of his death in Hawaii in 1779, he was the most successful European explorer of his era. **NE**

a small garrison there at Port Egmont. Just four months after returning home, and now under a new commander, *Endeavour* was sent to reprovision the isolated outpost. In all, the ship made three voyages to the Falklands until finally, after failing survey in 1775, HMB *Endeavour* was sold out of the navy.

Endeavour made one voyage, to Archangel in northern Russia, before the outbreak of the American Revolution changed the vessel's career path forever.

Britain's response to the uprising in its American colonies was to send a large infantry contingent to reinforce its existing troops in America, and *Endeavour,* now renamed *Lord Sandwich,* was one of hundreds of ships chartered to transport the troops across the Atlantic.

It was in America that the ship finally ended its days — one of over a dozen transports deliberately sunk to impede a French naval attack on Newport, Rhode Island, in August 1778. **NE**

What's it like to sail on *Endeavour*?

WHEN MANY people first see the *Endeavour* replica, they question how the ship sails, with its bluff bow pushing along so much water. In addition, many believe that square-rigged ships can only sail downwind and must be slow and uncomfortable. The reality is surprisingly different.

When putting to sea on the replica, the first thing you notice is the comfortable motion as the ship steadily rolls, pitches and scends (rises again) on the swell. The masts swing in wide, gentle arcs against the sky, whispers of wind filling the billowing canvas. The ship heels over comfortably as the helmsman puts a bit of helm on to check its tendency to gripe (to turn into the wind, or 'round up'; this is what sailors call 'weather helm'). This only takes one or two spokes of helm.

The hard work of setting the sails is soon forgotten once we sit back and admire the beauty of the vessel under full sail. There is the creaking and sighing of the ship's timbers, the slight rapping of reef points against their sails far above and the occasional slap from a wave striking. Below decks, nothing can be heard other than the creaking hull and the gurgle of water passing along the ship's sides.

There were very good reasons why the British Admiralty and James Cook chose this old coal-hauler, built in Whitby on England's north-east coast, for a long voyage to the South Seas. The original collier, the *Earl of Pembroke*, was built to be managed by a small crew, strong and seaworthy enough to survive the rough, shallow North Sea and occasional groundings, nimble enough to get in and out of coastal ports, and capacious enough to carry a viable cargo. In James Cook's case, there was room enough for supplies and a cargo of sailors, scientists and marines.

When balanced with the right sails for the conditions, the replica *Endeavour* leads itself, with minimal input from the helmsman. At times the helm may need no adjustment for up to half an hour, and then it might only need half a spoke (1/20th of a turn on the ship's wheel). The ship only needs a slight breeze to make enough way to gain steerage, which occurs when making about one knot through the water. This surprises some people, since the tall rudder is very narrow, designed to create the least amount of drag. The ship can be kept on course in as little as five knots of breeze. **AL**

> **'Sailing on *Endeavour* is all about learning 18th-century sailing skills in a 21st-century world. It's great to escape our busy lives and enjoy the open blue waters, fresh sea air and marine life.'**
> **Amy Spets**
> *Endeavour* replica shipkeeper

LEFT The *Endeavour* replica carries both professional and amateur crew and offers a rare chance to learn how to sail 18th-century style.
ANMM image

BELOW The *Endeavour* replica sails comfortably in a force-9 gale in Bass Strait in 1994, during one of its first voyages.
ANMM image

What's what on board?

The *Endeavour* replica's home port is the Australian National Maritime Museum. When not voyaging, it is a living history museum that is visited by thousands of people each year.

RIGGING
Endeavour has about 30 km of rigging. Standing rigging supports the mast and is made of a natural fibre called manila with polyester added for extra strength and safety. Running rigging (about 7 km) is used to control the sails and is mostly polypropylene.

TOPS
These platforms spread the rigging to help support the higher sections of the masts. They also enable the crew to work more safely at height.

SHIP'S BOATS
Endeavour carried a longboat (its primary work boat, and the largest) and four other boats.

GREAT CABIN
Normally the captain's cabin, but on Cook's voyage it was used to store botanical specimens.

QUARTER BADGE WINDOW
One on each side of the ship, allowing light and air into the Great Cabin.

RUDDER
Connected to the wheel, and the means of steering the vessel. *Endeavour*'s rudder is made of Western Australian jarrah.

PINTLE & GUDGEON
(not visible). These bronze fittings are connected to the rudder.

BOARDING LADDER
A ladder fixed to the hull, which sailors used to board the ship from its boats.

PARBUCKLING RAILS
Two vertical timbers on which barrels were rolled up and loaded on board.

BLOCKS
Used to control the running rigging, to give extra purchase when pulling.

SHROUDS & RATLINES
Shrouds are vertical ropes that support the masts. Ratlines are horizontal ropes that the crew use as a ladder to reach the masts and spars.

SAILS
(not pictured)
The replica has 17 sails in its basic rig, with a few more for light airs. Cook's *Endeavour* carried up to 30 sails.

BOWSPRIT & JIBBOOM
Increase sail area by allowing the sail(s) to protrude past the bow. Also help to allay the ship's tendency to turn up into the wind.

Ship model of
HMB *Endeavour*,
scale ½ inch to 1 foot.
Powerhouse Collection
H8855 Purchased 1970.
Photo Jane Townsend

ANCHORS
(not indicated)
Endeavour carries two bower anchors, 2 tonnes each; two stream anchors, 1.2 tonnes each; a kedge anchor, 600 kg; and a small coasting anchor.

FLAT BOTTOM
Adds strength to the ship's construction so it can sit safely and upright on the sea floor at low tide. Also allows ease of access when loading.

WALE
A structural member running right around the ship to hold it together. *Endeavour*'s wale is jarrah, 15 cm thick.

HOLD
Storage space for cargo. *Endeavour* could carry about 200 tonnes.

BLUFF BOW
Allows the vessel to ride over waves rather than through them, thus shipping less water and keeping the cargo dry.

Endeavour, Cook and 18th-century geopolitics

Secret orders

Publicly, *Endeavour*'s voyage to the South Pacific was for the purpose of observing the transit of Venus. Privately, Cook was issued with additional 'secret' orders that required him to search for a great continent, long speculated by geographers to exist in the southern hemisphere. The orders required him to sail south from Tahiti as far as latitude 40°, and then if nothing was found, to continue sailing west between latitudes 35° and 40° until either finding the southern continent or locating the east coast of the land that had been named New Zealand by the Dutch, following Abel Tasman's landfall on its west coast over a century earlier.

If Cook succeeded in finding a southern continent, the orders required him to carefully record the location of prominent bays, headlands and anchorages, but also to note the quality of the soil, the botanical and mineral resources, and the 'Genius, Temper, Disposition and Number of the Natives'. He was to attempt to cultivate 'Friendship and Alliance' with them, but to be always 'upon [his] guard against Accidents'. The orders allowed Cook freedom to decide how best to return home, and almost as an afterthought ordered him to take possession of any islands not yet discovered by Europeans.

Cook sailed south from Tahiti as directed, but found no sign of the supposed continent before sighting the coast of New Zealand in early October 1769. His first landing in New Zealand was at a place he named Poverty Bay (now called Tūranganui-a-Kiwa) because he found nothing useful to supply the ship. The landing went badly and several Māori people were killed there. While this first engagement was a failure, a welcome surprise was the discovery that the Māori understood a Polynesian priest named Tupaia, who had joined *Endeavour* in Tahiti, when he spoke to them in his own language. This was a great help during the six months that Cook spent charting New Zealand.

On 1 April 1770, the ship left Cape Farewell, sailing west to seek the east coast of New Holland. On 19 April land was sighted at what is now called Point Hicks, in Victoria. Heading north, Cook landed at Botany Bay one week later. **NE**

LEFT Cook's secret orders from the Admiralty. National Library of Australia nla.obj-229111770

RIGHT *The Observatory, Point Venus, Otahytey* [Tahiti], George Tobin, 1792. State Library of New South Wales (FL16066978)

BRITAIN EMERGED as a clear winner at the end of the global conflict known as the Seven Years War (1756–63). Regarded as the first global conflict, the war engulfed Britain and France, and their respective allies in North America, the Caribbean, Europe and India. When it finally ended, Britain found itself not only in control of Canada, French Louisiana and Florida, but more importantly, it had unrivalled control of the sea.

While Spain and Portugal were well established in the Americas, and the Dutch controlled much of the trade in Southeast Asia, Robert Clive's victory at the Battle of Plassey in 1757 had laid the foundation for the English East India Company's rule in Bengal and, ultimately, British control of the entire subcontinent. In China, the Emperor Qianlong maintained a closed

door to the West, restricting European traders to the port of Canton. In the Atlantic, British colonies such as Jamaica, Barbados and Antigua were increasingly turning to sugar production over tobacco and coffee — further expanding the use of slave labour.

It was against this background that Britain sent Commodore John Byron in charge of the ships *Dolphin* and *Tamar* to the Pacific in 1764, to explore the potential territory, resources and trade routes in a vast area of the globe largely unknown to Europe. The mission was not a success. Byron claimed the Falkland Islands and located a few islands in the Pacific, but is best remembered for completing the circumnavigation in just two years. The Admiralty was not impressed, and soon after its return, *Dolphin* was again sent to the Pacific, this time under the command of Samuel Wallis and accompanied by HMS *Swallow*. During this voyage, Wallis was the first European to encounter Tahiti, and he returned to England in 1768, just months before James Cook and *Endeavour* were due to depart. Wallis's glowing report of the secure anchorage of Matavai Bay convinced the Royal Society to make Tahiti the Pacific base for its observation of the transit of Venus, and there, on 3 June 1769, the astronomer Charles Green and Cook observed the transit.

Later in June, Cook and Banks spent six days circumnavigating the island, alternately walking or using one of *Endeavour*'s boats to explore and chart Tahiti's coastline. On the chart that he produced, Cook gave the name Point Venus to the prominent point where he established the tent observatory. NE

Observing the transit of Venus

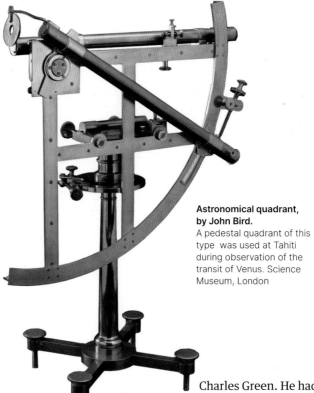

Astronomical quadrant, by John Bird.
A pedestal quadrant of this type was used at Tahiti during observation of the transit of Venus. Science Museum, London

AS EARLY as 1716, the astronomer Edmund Halley had described how the transit of the planet Venus across the face of the sun could be used to calculate the distance of the earth from the sun. This calculation would help scientists to better understand the relative size of the solar system, and also benefit seafarers, who largely depended on observations of the sun to navigate.

Transits of Venus are rare, occurring in pairs eight years apart, every 105-120 years. The calculation depended on the combined observations and timing of Venus's movement across the face of the sun from observatories across the world, and Halley had recommended that observatories be set up for the 1761 transit in places as widely spread as Hudson Bay in Canada, Norway, and the Molucca Islands (part of modern Indonesia). In fact, observations were made from many more places in 1761, but the overall results were unsatisfactory. The 1769 transit thus represented the last opportunity for more than 100 years (the next would be 1874) to resolve the issue.

The chief observer for the transit, as designated by the Royal Society, was Charles Green. He had been an assistant to several Astronomers Royal at the Royal Observatory, Greenwich, before being appointed for the *Endeavour* voyage. Despite the difficulties Green, Cook and Solander had in timing the transit, the mathematician Thomas Hornby, by using their results and those from other 1769 observations, was able to calculate the distance from the earth to the sun with surprising accuracy.

Cook noted in his journal on 3 June 1769:

This day proved as favourable to our purpose as we could wish. Not a cloud was to be seen the whole day, and the air was perfectly clear, so that we had every advantage we could desire in observing the whole passage of the planet Venus over the Sun's disk ... Dr Solander observed as well as Mr Green and myself, and we differed from one another in observing the times of the contact much more than could be expected.

Charles Green died at sea after *Endeavour* left Batavia. Cook named Green Island (Wunyami), just north of Cairns, Queensland, after him. **NE**

Seven weeks after leaving Tahiti, and having, according to his secret orders, searched but found no sign of a new continent, Cook sighted part of New Zealand's north island in early October 1769. New Zealand was already known to Europeans, as the Dutch explorer Abel Tasman had mapped a part of the east coast in 1642.

Before leaving Tahiti, Cook had agreed to take on board Tupaia, a Polynesian priest who had proved useful in negotiations between the Europeans and the Tahitians. He also demonstrated a surprising knowledge of the Pacific islands and happily drew a map showing around 70, with names and their relative direction from Tahiti. An even greater surprise, however, was revealed when, on one of Cook's first encounters with Māori, it was discovered that they understood Tupaia when he spoke to them in his own language.

Thereafter, Tupaia accompanied Cook and botanists Joseph Banks and Daniel Solander whenever they went ashore, and his presence was an undoubted boon during the six months that *Endeavour* spent in New Zealand.

Cook spent most of that time exploring the North Island, anchoring frequently to take on wood and water, to trade with the Māori, or to allow Banks and Solander to botanise. The ship attracted much attention, and the European sailors were especially appreciative of the skilled workmanship evident in the magnificent Māori canoes they encountered.

In early January 1770 Cook discovered the anchorage he named Ship Cove, at the mouth of a deep sound (now known as Queen Charlotte Sound). Over a period of three weeks, *Endeavour's* carpenters careened the ship and carried out minor repairs, readying it for the next stage of the voyage. The crew also brought aboard stone ballast collected from the shore.

It was also at Ship Cove that Cook had wooden posts erected, bearing the ship's name and date, and where on a small adjacent island he took formal possession of the sound and 'adjacent lands in the name and for the use of His Majesty'.

Cook conducted the survey of New Zealand's South Island in just seven weeks, never anchoring until he finally again reached the strait separating the two main islands.

Cook's secret orders allowed him to decide his homeward route. Judging it too late in the season to attempt returning via Cape Horn, he headed west.

On 19 April 1770, having crossed the Tasman Sea, Cook and his men became the first Europeans to sight the east coast of the land known as New Holland. Cook gave the name Point Hicks to the first point of land sighted. Based on existing outlines of New Holland, Cook almost certainly expected it would take several months following the long coast north before he might find himself in waters already explored by Europeans. What he couldn't anticipate was the entirely new world that *Endeavour* was about to enter, and the challenges that would confront all those aboard on the Great Barrier Reef. **NE**

On 19 April 1770, Cook and his men became the first Europeans to sight the east coast of New Holland

Māori trading a crayfish with Joseph Banks, 1769.
This is Tahitian high priest and navigator Tupaia's only known drawing of New Zealand.
© British Library Board. Shelfmark Add MS 15508. f.12

Thinkers, ambassadors & artists

THERE WERE no scientists aboard HM Bark *Endeavour*. In fact, the word 'scientist' was not coined until 1833 — just four years before the death of the final crew member from Cook's first Pacific voyage.

Endeavour did boast ambassadors of knowledge, however. In their time they were known as 'learned gentlemen' or 'natural philosophers'.

Some were driven by curiosity about the world around them, or beyond the known horizon. Others saw a path to prestige through collecting and publishing new facts or proposing systems for organising and interpreting nature. While many sought to honour the grandeur of their God's creation, others paid tribute to a new god: reason.

In Europe and the colonised Americas, the late 1700s was known as the Age of Enlightenment. The universe was no longer to be understood through faith and tradition, but would instead be tested by observation and experiment. In Britain, the centre of Enlightenment thinking was the Royal Society, an independent scientific academy founded in 1660. And in 1768, one of its youngest stars was Joseph Banks.

Joseph Banks: genus and genius

Born in 1743, Banks was the handsome and inquisitive son of a wealthy family. Many subjects fascinated him, but his heart was planted in botany. Educated at the exclusive Harrow School and Eton College, he later attended Oxford University, where his focus was natural history. If not 'science' in the modern sense, natural history entailed describing plants, animals and minerals, then considering how they might relate to each other.

Upon learning of Cook's mission, Banks leapt at the chance to encounter novel organisms and environments. Supported by his fortune and endorsed by the Royal Society, he invested an estimated £10,000 (about $3 million in today's terms) in books, instruments, accoutrements and people. His staff of eight comprised fellow philosophers, artists and servants. As the voyage progressed, their collections blossomed and *Endeavour's* hold swelled with specimens new to European eyes. These included flora, fauna, geological samples and cultural objects from the many First Nations peoples they met.

Perhaps the most telling moment of Banks' three years aboard *Endeavour* came on 22 November 1769. Moored in the Wairau River in Aotearoa New Zealand, the vessel attracted many Māori people in canoes. Keen to collect examples of their clothing and weapons, Banks found that what the Māori most wanted in return was European paper. And, in a sense, paper was his most important commodity. Through paper, Banks consulted charts, read books, kept diaries, recorded observations, made sketches, wrote letters and proposed ideas. Paper made his reputation and ensured his legacy.

Surprisingly, therefore, paper was also central to Banks' greatest disappointment. Over the three-year voyage, most of his team died. Each loss added to the workload of those remaining to catalogue and illustrate the ever-growing trove of specimens. Increasingly, artists Sydney Parkinson and Herman Diedrich Spöring could only complete sketches and rough notes, intending their work to be finalised at a later date — then they also died. When Banks arrived back in England, he spent a fortune preparing a florilegium — an exhaustively illustrated catalogue of the plants observed on the *Endeavour* voyage. But, short of funds and diverted by his many commitments, the project faltered and Banks' *Florilegium* was not printed until the 1980s.

But well before his own death in 1820, Joseph Banks was recognised as a genius of natural history. In 1782, an entire genus of hardy shrubs from Australia was named in his honour — *Banksia*. It became one among an orchard of honours and appointments that Banks harvested in the wake of *Endeavour*.

**Daniel Solander:
fangs and flowers**

In theory, the Enlightenment knew no borders. Europeans and colonial Americans believed they belonged to a 'Republic of Letters' — a community of scholars dedicated to the exchange of knowledge, regardless of nationality. In reality, it was never that utopian, but Banks was well connected and brought two foreigners aboard what was, after all, a British naval vessel.

The most eminent was Daniel Solander, a protégé of the highly influential Swedish naturalist Carl Linnaeus. Solander had earned the enormous task of arranging the British Museum's collection of natural history specimens when he met Banks, and they became great friends. Aboard *Endeavour*, Solander prepared detailed descriptions of the specimens gathered by the expedition.

Words were his tools. He systematically recorded physical details such as location, size, shape, weight, colours and distinctive features, from fangs to flowers. Written in the scholarly language of Latin, these descriptions were critical to deciding each organism's place in nature. But Solander — and many naturalists after him — struggled with the 'kanguru'. They learned its name from the Guugu Yimithirr people of far north Queensland, but exactly which species of kangaroo the *Endeavour* party collected in 1770 remains a mystery to this day.

A singular Animal called Kangaroo found on the Coast of New Holland.

Sydney Parkinson: artistry and dysentery

Perhaps the greatest scientific tragedy of Cook's voyage was the death, late in the journey, of Sydney Parkinson. Although a competent illustrator before *Endeavour* departed in 1768, Parkinson's skills, ambitions and accomplishments escalated with each month at sea. Both his scope and productivity increased after landscape artist and portraitist Alexander Buchan died following an epileptic seizure in Tahiti in 1769.

Parkinson's burden was prodigious. He had to accurately capture the shape and details of every new specimen, often via rough sketches made in the field. He was then to transform these preliminaries into a finished drawing or painting, whether a delicate bloom or an elaborate cultural performance.

As the voyage stretched out, scenes and specimens proliferated. Overworked and exhausted, Parkinson contracted dysentery — a diarrhoea disease — after *Endeavour* reached Batavia (now Jakarta) in 1771. He was just 26 when he died at sea. Although thousands of his sketches remained unfinished, a vast number were later developed by artists employed by Banks, forming the core of his astounding *Florilegium.*

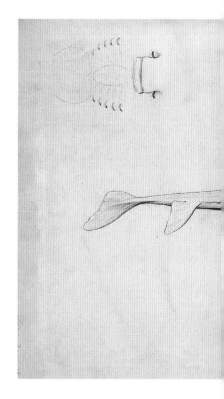

Herman Diedrich Spöring: nature and culture

Although employed primarily to assist Banks, Finnish natural philosopher Herman Diedrich Spöring also demonstrated superlative drafting talents. Assisting Sydney Parkinson after Andrew Buchan's death, Spöring provided highly detailed technical drawings of creatures and cultural objects such as watercraft. Perhaps the finest were the two stingrays that he recorded in an Australian inlet initially known as Stingray Bay, but soon after renamed by Cook to Botany Bay. **PH**

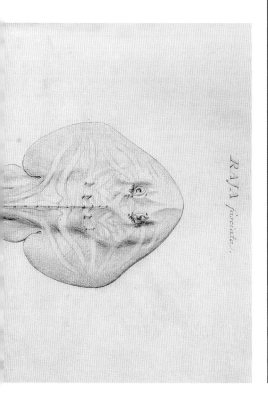

Arranging the world

When *Endeavour* finally docked back in England in 1771, its hold boasted 3,600 dried plant specimens, more than a third never previously recorded by Western naturalists. Although many seeds did not survive, later that year 14 species were already germinating in English soil, including Australian gum trees and mānuka myrtle from Aotearoa New Zealand. But why would Britain's navy risk crews and vessels to collect vines and vegetables?

Many Enlightenment scholars viewed nature as an endless bounty provided for human exploitation. Sailors were astute observers of plants that added nutritional, medicinal or culinary value in local cultures around the world. The Royal Navy, for instance, was delighted when Cook's first voyage revealed the incredible versatility of the New Zealand flax plant (*Phormium tenax*), which promised to make stronger ropes than the hemp then in use. In 1774, on his second Pacific journey, Cook proposed that the tall, straight and strong pine trees on Norfolk Island would form excellent ships' masts.

In addition to finding such botanical riches, Europeans also sought to transplant them. The centuries-old spice trade had demonstrated how profitable it might be to establish pepper or nutmeg, for instance, closer to their main commercial markets. After the *Endeavour* voyage, Banks transformed London's Kew Gardens into a centre where 'curious or valuable plants' from around the globe were cultivated. Likewise, in 1787 he despatched diverse seeds for herbs, grains, vegetables, berries and fruits to the new colony that Britain planned to establish in New South Wales.

But new knowledge about plants was also seen as a good

thing in itself. In Enlightenment terms, it produced order and reason, where once there had been chaos and ignorance. This process was both intellectually and spiritually uplifting. As a major branch of natural history, botany was easily accessible and infinitely varied. The process of describing plants could be an amateur pursuit for priests or ladies, while learned gentlemen amassed vast collections and shared information via letters, lectures and publications.

What transformed natural history — especially botany — was the work of Carl Linnaeus. From the 1730s this Swedish doctor created a system of organising organisms via a pair of names, such as *Banksia serrata*. The first name, the genus, grouped similar plants or animals together, whether cats or cacti. The second was specific to organisms within a genus that had unique characteristics, so it was known as the species name. This Linnaean or 'binomial' system was championed by Banks and Solander, since it offered a harmonious and universal way of arranging the world into neat categories. **PH**

Endeavour surveys Australia's east coast

Endeavour sighted the east coast of Australia on 19 April 1770 at latitude 38° south and sailed north over a period of four months until reaching Possession Island (Bedhan Lag) in Torres Strait. After landing there, Cook raised the English flag and:

took possession of the whole eastern coast ...by the name of New Wales [later changed to New South Wales] together with all the bays, harbours, rivers, and islands situated upon the coast ...

The voyage along the east coast covered some 3,700 kilometres, during which Cook and his men charted and named prominent landmarks and other features. Some names referenced remarkable landforms (Mount Dromedary, Pigeon House); other places he named to alert future mariners (Mount Warning, Point Danger). Some were named for dates in the religious calendar (the Whitsunday Islands) or strange occurrences (Magnetical Island), but many more after British Admirals (Cape Howe), statesmen (Cape Grafton) and royalty (Cape York).

As a sailing ship dependent on wind and tide, *Endeavour* was sometimes forced to anchor, particularly after entering the Great Barrier Reef, but the occasions on which Cook landed to explore the country were few.

He first anchored on the east coast at Botany Bay (Kamay) in late April 1770, where he and his men first encountered some of the Indigenous inhabitants of the country, and where Joseph Banks and Daniel Solander were able to collect examples of the flora and fauna. Cook mapped and named the bay (originally Stingray Bay, soon changed to Botany Bay) during the eight days the ship remained there, but then did not go ashore again until Bustard Bay (23 May).

A few days later he landed a little further north, hoping to find a place to clean the bottom of the ship. The lack of any fresh water source in the area caused him to change his mind and he named the place Thirsty Sound. Cook went ashore again at Cape Grafton (Yarrabah) looking for fresh water (10 June), but although he found several streams, none was accessible to *Endeavour*'s boats. It was very nearly the last place that Cook went ashore, for late the following day the ship struck Endeavour Reef.

After 24 harrowing hours the ship floated free, and the urgent need to carry out repairs resulted in *Endeavour*'s six-week stay at Endeavour River (Waalumbaal Birri). The interlude provided time for a more prolonged encounter between the Europeans and the Indigenous people of the area, which, despite misunderstandings, seems to have had a profound effect on Cook and Banks.

The final leg of Cook's voyage up the east coast after leaving Endeavour River was both difficult and dangerous. Confronted by the prospect of reefs barring his progress, he anchored at Point Lookout (11 August) in search of a way out of the maze of reefs. The following day he took one of the ship's boats and landed at Lizard Island (Jiigurru) further off the coast. From its summit, he saw a passage through which, a day later, *Endeavour* sailed into the open sea.

However, the relief of once again having sea room was short lived; judging it his duty to continue the survey of the coast, at great danger to the ship and all aboard, Cook re-entered the reef a few days later (17 August). Cook knew that he had been lucky to escape destruction on the reef, but his success meant that he was able to continue his survey, ultimately leaving only a relatively small section of the coast for later colonial navigators to chart.

Cook's landing at Possession Island effectively completed his survey of the east coast, but he made one final landing at Booby Island (24 August) before sailing west into waters already known to Europe. **NE**

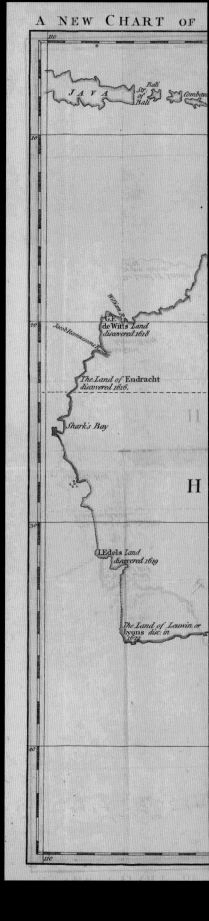

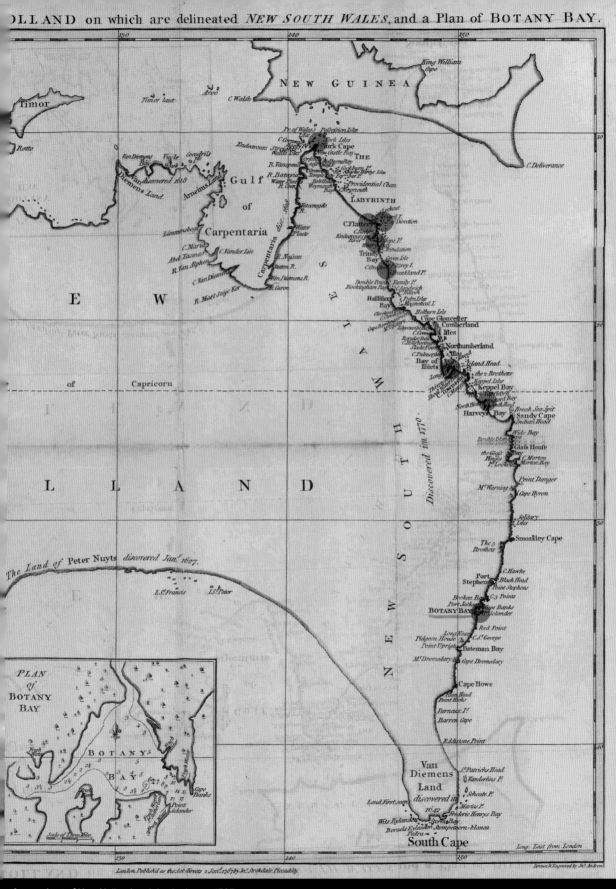

Six weeks at Endeavour River

As we went ashore about the top of High Water we not only started our water [emptied the fresh water barrels], but threw overboard our guns, iron and stone ballast, casks, hoop staves, oil jars, decayed stores etc. — Endeavour journal

WHEN, ON 11 June 1770, *Endeavour* struck a coral reef during the night, the ship, its people and the entire success and achievements of the expedition hung in the balance. The Great Barrier Reef stretches from just north of Bundaberg to the Torres Strait, starting as solitary coral islands in the south, but gradually forming a maze of interlinking reefs further north. Stuck on a reef more than 20 kilometres offshore, with the nearest European settlement more than 2,000 kilometres distant, Cook had to refloat the ship before the weather changed and *Endeavour* was pounded to pieces.

To do this, the ship needed to be made lighter in the hope that, with increased buoyancy, it would float free on the next high tide. In fact, *Endeavour* remained aground for a further 24 hours until it was successfully

Concretion removed from one of the cannons recovered from Endeavour Reef. It bears an impression of the royal cypher with the stylised initials GR (George Rex) and a crown. ANMM Collection 00029235

Conserving *Endeavour's* kentledge

Artefacts recovered from marine archaeological sites pose a challenge to conservators. When these objects first sink to the ocean floor, they are vulnerable to chemical, mechanical and biological attack. As the years and decades pass, the rate at which they decay slows, and eventually they reach a state of equilibrium with their environment. However, this balance is lost when artefacts are removed from the water. For metal objects, exposure to the air

can rapidly turn an important piece of history into a meaningless pile of dust. It's the conservator's role to preserve artefacts by arresting active deterioration while maintaining evidence of their use and age.

The cannons, munitions and kentledge (iron ballast) that Cook jettisoned from HMB *Endeavour* in 1770 provide us with examples of metallic objects that have been successfully preserved. These objects

were recovered by archaeologists in 1969 and treated by conservators soon after. Their treatment involved chipping away marine concretions, removing harmful salts and applying a protective clear coating.

Inspection of the kentledge in 2019, in the lead-up to the 250th anniversary of Cook's arrival on the east coast of Australia, revealed some minor ongoing deterioration. The coating applied to the objects had hauled free with the aid of anchors rowed out into deeper water. The amount of water entering the damaged ship then threatened to overcome the pumps, and with the crew working desperately to stem the flow with an old sail drawn under the hull, there was no time to try to raise the guns or other jettisoned material. It was all left on the reef.

Once the leaks had been brought under control, Cook's next problem was to find a place on the coast where the ship's carpenters could repair the damage, and he must have breathed a sigh of relief when a protected river entrance was discovered, and *Endeavour* was secured within it a few days later. Cook named it Endeavour River, and the ship remained there for six weeks — the longest stop that Cook made in Australia, and one that produced some important outcomes.

Perhaps the most important was the opportunity the extended delay provided Cook and his men to engage with the local Indigenous people, the Guugu Yimithirr, who despite being offended by some of the actions of the Europeans, acted peaceably and with great tolerance.

The delay also gave Joseph Banks and Daniel Solander the opportunity to botanise, and the collections they made at Endeavour River were the largest they gathered in Australia. Also at Endeavour River, Lieutenant Gore shot a kangaroo, the first ever seen closely by Europeans. Sydney Parkinson sketched the animal, and its skin was taken back to England, where the artist George Stubbs used it as the basis for his rather rat-like portrait of the animal.

Kentledge and cannons: lost and found

And what of the objects thrown overboard at Endeavour Reef?

In 1969, in the lead-up to the bicentenary of Cook's voyage along the east coast of Australia, an expedition was funded by the Academy of Natural Sciences, Philadelphia. It principally focused on collecting marine specimens but also searched for *Endeavour*'s guns. An aerial survey of Endeavour Reef located a magnetic anomaly that, on investigation, proved to be the long-lost iron cannons and ballast. The expedition recovered all six of the cannons thrown overboard in 1770, along with all the iron, and some stone ballast.

Eighteenth-century ships such as *Endeavour* carried internal ballast deep in the hold in the form of stone shingle or elongated blocks of iron that could be added or removed to maintain the stability of the vessel. A naval vessel of *Endeavour*'s size would normally have carried 50 tonnes of iron ballast (known as kentledge), but given the weight of stores it would have to carry for its voyage, Cook chose to reduce the amount of iron ballast, planning to load local stone ballast whenever necessary.

The six cannons and the iron ballast were treated by conservators in time for the 200th anniversary, and in a gesture acknowledging the significance of Cook's *Endeavour* to several countries, the Australian government gave a cannon each to the United Kingdom, New Zealand and the Academy of Natural Sciences, Philadelphia. The three remaining guns are now in Australian cultural institutions. NE

aged and hardened and had stopped performing its protective function. This presented conservators with the interesting problem of how to remove the stubborn but compromised coating without damaging the objects' surface or patina.

Testing led them to develop a process by which an industrial laser was used to weaken the old coating and dry-ice blasting was then used to remove it. Once complete, a corrosion converting solution and a modern, clear coating were applied. As a result, the cause of deterioration has been addressed, signs of the object's age have been kept and a new coating has been applied that we hope will protect the kentledge for another 50 years. **NF, JF**

LEFT AND ABOVE Kentledge (iron ballast) recovered from Endeavour Reef. ANMM Collection

RIGHT The kentledge undergoing conservation in 2019. ANMM image

Contact and consequences

**For Aboriginal and Torres Strait Islander people,
Endeavour's legacy is one of dispossession, disease and
cultural repression. Professor John Maynard reflects on
the repercussions of Cook's voyage and decisions.**

IN RAISING the British flag on Possession Island
in the Torres Strait in August 1770 and claiming
the east coast of Australia in the name of his king
and country, James Cook unleashed cataclysmic
consequences upon Aboriginal people of the
Australian continent.

As an Aboriginal historian, I cannot but
recognise, in the wake of this single event, the
horrific impact and cultural destruction that
would explode across the continent in the
decades ahead. At its height, the Aboriginal
population would teeter on near-complete
annihilation through disease, warfare and severe
government policies. I also recognise that it
would be completely unrealistic to think that
we would have remained immune to outside
invasion and its impact even if Cook had not
stepped ashore in 1770.

I admire James Cook as a skilled navigator
and an inspiring leader of his crews. Cook's
working-class upbringing instilled in him a
capacity to view the world through a different
lens, and he was instrumental in fostering loyalty
in the crews that sailed under him. In 2014 I went
on board the *Endeavour* replica at the Australian
National Maritime Museum, and I was struck by
what an achievement it was to sail such a tiny
craft across so vast a distance and through some
terrifying seas.

But what of his journey to Botany Bay and
his orders in relation to Aboriginal people?
Cook had received secret instructions from the
British Admiralty, and as such from the Crown
itself, which advised that in the event he found
the continent, he should chart its coasts, obtain
information about its people, cultivate their

friendship and alliance, and appropriate any
convenient trading posts in the King's name.

But clearly Cook did not open up any
meaningful dialogue or discussion, nor did he
gain any consent in claiming the entire east
coast of the continent. In this, he was in direct
violation of his orders from the Crown.

In fact, the evidence that can be gleaned from
his own records clearly implies the opposite: as
Cook sets down in his journal, 'all [the Aboriginal
people] seem'd to want was for us to be gone'.[1]
There was no welcome mat of consent rolled out.

The arrogance of Cook's actions in claiming
possession of the continent without any alliance
with, or consent from, the owners, and the
ignorance on his part that this suggests, stands
in stark contrast to his glowing written record
which speaks of a paradise of equality:

> [I]n reality they are far more happier than
> we Europeans; being wholy unacquainted not
> only with the superfluous but the necessary
> conveniencies so much sought after in Europe,
> they are happy in not knowing the use of them.
> They live in a Tranquillity which is not disturb'd
> by the Inequality of Condition: The Earth and
> sea of their own accord furnishes them with all
> things necessary for life … they live in a warm
> and fine Climate and enjoy a very wholsome Air.

Communities in south-eastern Australia,
where Cook had direct impact, have maintained
and built Cook into their understandings of
the past and their everyday language. Sandy
Cameron, a Yagirr Elder on the north coast of
New South Wales, was interviewed by linguist
Terry Crowley in 1973 and recorded a song in her
language of Cook's visit. Cameron explained:

> I told this fellow there was this Captain Cook.
> He was the King of the tribe and had all this tin
> stuff and plonk and tobacco. All the dark people

Black bastards are coming by Gordon Syron, 2013.
Syron's work shifts persectives, imagining black soldiers
approaching the shore, flying an Aboriginal flag, and firing
upon white 'natives'. ANMM Collection 00008521

European views

had a look. He's a wuyirribin ... wuyirribin that's a boat ... That's a ship coming in ... and they say warrayi who this ship coming in? And Captain Cook shouldn't have bowed the boat with the bush ... just as much to say he's a friend, friend coming in. He jumped in a little boat ... when he paddled in, he left the big boat outside ... big sailing you know? Walked in waving, the chief of the tribe went to them with boomerang and spears. 'No ...' he said 'wanha, wanha STOP'.

In stating firmly that 'Captain Cook shouldn't have bowed the boat with the bush' and that the old chief had called out 'No ... *wanha, wanha* STOP', the message conveyed is that Cook and his crew initially should not have come ashore.

Cook did not open up any meaningful discussion, nor did he gain any consent in claiming the entire east coast of the continent.

The Yuin people on the south coast of New South Wales retained oral memories that recognise the lack of any formal consent or contact with Cook. In Umburra Cultural Centre's manuscript 'View from the Mountain', they noted that 'Cook's maps were very good, but they did not show us our names for places. He didn't ask us.'

Aboriginal people across New South Wales lampooned Cook. Ray Kelly told me that as a kid on 'the Mish' (mission) at Armidale, he knew older people, who when they spotted a welfare officer, or even an unknown 'gubba' (white person), would say, 'Lookey, lookey, here comes Cookey'. The humour and retained bitter memory of James Cook, and what he represents, remain etched deeply within the fabric of many Aboriginal communities on the east coast of Australia. Cook is still at the top of the heap of historical bogeymen. JM

1. James Cook, Journal of HMS *Endeavour*, 1768–1771 [manuscript], entry for Monday 30 April 1770. National Library of Australia http://nla.gov.au/nla.obj-229041389

In New Zealand, the common language of the Polynesian priest Tupaia and the Māori inhabitants proved of enormous benefit. It facilitated trade and access to the land, and enhanced the Europeans' understanding of Māori culture. In New Holland, by contrast, no common language existed between *Endeavour*'s crew and the Indigenous people. Although Cook's overall impression of the Indigenous people was positive, encounters were still marked by misunderstanding and bloodshed.

At Botany Bay, *Endeavour*'s first stop in Australia, Cook and his men were surprised by the apparent lack of interest the Eora people showed in the ship's arrival, but they could appreciate the courage of two men who confronted the landing party, as Joseph Banks recorded in his journal:

They called to us very loud in a harsh sounding language of which neither us or [Tupaia] understood a word, shaking their lances and menacing, in all appearance resolved to dispute our landing to the utmost though they were but two and we 30 or 40 at least.

Sadly, this first encounter ended violently when the landing party fired and wounded one of the men, who after throwing their spears, withdrew into the bush. From then, the Eora very reasonably avoided contact. During the eight days that *Endeavour* remained anchored in the bay, the only other engagements were haphazard and unintentional, leading Banks, quite unreasonably, to regard the local inhabitants as 'rank cowards'.

Sailors from *Endeavour* share their catch of fish with Aboriginal people of *Endeavour* River. Plate 8 from a French book titled *Nouvelle Bibliotheque des Voyages Tome 2*. ANMM Collection 00037896

Endeavour's enforced stay of six weeks at Endeavour River provided a far longer period for engagement between the Europeans and Guugu Yimithirr people. It was generally marked by small, peaceful encounters prior to a serious disagreement triggered over turtles.

Throughout the ship's stay in the river, Cook had sent out parties to hunt or fish. On the day of the incident, several turtles laid out on Endeavour's deck became the cause of a quickly escalating dispute when a group of Aboriginal men visited the ship. When their sign-language request for a turtle was rejected, they soon left the ship and lit a grass fire that threatened to destroy some stores and equipment left ashore. The damage to the goods was contained, but only after a

Guugu Yimithirr man was wounded. Despite this violence, the situation was later reconciled by the actions of an Indigenous elder. Joseph Banks described what was, in effect, the first recorded act of reconciliation between Europeans and the Indigenous inhabitants of Australia:

The little old man now came forward to us carrying in his hand a lance without a point... We beckoned to him to come: he then spoke to the others who all laid their lances against a tree and leaving them came forwards likewise and soon came quite to us. They had with them it seems 3 strangers who wanted to see the ship .... The strangers were presented to us by name and we gave them such trinkets as we had about us ...

The trinkets were of no interest, leading Banks to later reflect:

From them appear how small are the real wants of human nature, which we Europeans have increased to an excess which would certainly appear incredible to these people could they be told.

Though frustrated by the inability to communicate verbally with the Guugu Yimithirr people, Banks was a keen observer and recorded a wealth of information about their culture – ranging from a small list of words, to descriptions of outrigger canoes, spears tipped with stingray barbs, and the scars and piercings he saw on many of the Indigenous men. **NE**

A case for repatriation

Two of the natives of New Holland, advancing to combat, engraving after a drawing by Sydney Parkinson, 1773. Published in *A journal of a voyage to the South Seas, in His Majesty's Ship the Endeavour.* ANMM Collection 00004423

The ownership and interpretation of Indigenous artefacts by Western institutions are increasingly contentious. Four spears stolen by the crew of HMB *Endeavour* in 1770 sit at the heart of the debate, as Matt Poll writes.

'... One of them, under cover of a shield, approached the boats and threw his gig [spear], and in return was wounded ...'
— A journal of the *Endeavour*, 28 April 1770

IN MARCH 2023, Trinity College, Cambridge, agreed to return four garrara (fishing spears) to the La Perouse Aboriginal community whose members are descendants of the people who watched *Endeavour* sail into Kamay (Botany Bay) in April 1770.

Aboriginal and Torres Strait Island people have long fought to influence how their cultures are represented and interpreted by Western institutions. The return of these spears, from the Cambridge Museum of Archaeology and Anthropology, acknowledges this fight and represents a significant turning point in the understanding of the *Endeavour* story.

These gararra extend back more than 250 years, to a foundational moment in the story of contact between First People and Europeans. They are among more than 40 gararra stolen by the crew of the *Endeavour* during its eight days in Kamay (Botany Bay). Ever since, they have been inaccessible to generations of Aboriginal and Torres Strait Island people — the owners of the spears, the keepers of their story.

The lineage of the gararra offers a rare glimpse into the pre-contact world of Sydney's Aboriginal past.

Fishing spears were an integral part of the daily life of Eora men in the greater Sydney basin. Women were also skilled fishers, but they preferred to fish from their watercraft in Sydney Harbour, using hooks ground from turban shell.

Fishing was one way in which Eora people demonstrated their superb knowledge of Sydney's sea country. Indigenous knowledge about local fishing conditions and locations was highly sought after by European members of the early colony of Port Jackson, as was their catch.

For more than 20 years, the La Perouse-based Gadhungal Research Group has negotiated with the Cambridge museum about the spears, which were given to Trinity College by the Earl of Sandwich (Cook's patron at the Admiralty) in 1771.

This discussion has brought a fascinating interpretive layer into how these moments from such a pivotal point of colonisation can be used to construct new and productive narratives of Australia's troubled relationship with its Aboriginal and Torres Strait Island past.

The gararra made a temporary return to Sydney in 2020, where they were shown at the University of Sydney's Chau Chak Wing Museum. They were exhibited not as examples of an inaccessible past, but alongside 50 contemporary examples of gararra made by Rod Mason, a senior Dharawal man and clan leader of the Gweagal community. This powerful demonstration of cultural continuity challenged the idea that museums should own and hold Aboriginal objects and stories that are not in the control of the Indigenous community. The spears will be returned and preserved on country at a new centre in Kamay.

The Gweagal spears are in themselves a beautiful mix of the botanic landscape of greater Sydney. Their shafts are made from abundant wattle found along the shores of Sydney Harbour and its inlets. The one to four prongs are mainly crafted from the flower stem of the xanthorrhoea, an iconic Australian species of flora also known as the grass tree. The Gadigal language group of Sydney derive their name from the plant: gadi means 'xanthorrhoea' and gal means 'people'. Xanthorrhoea resin, along with plant fibre or kangaroo sinew, binds the prongs to the shaft, while the tips of the prongs are embedded with beach shell or fish and marsupial teeth and bone.

Repatriation efforts, like those undertaken by the Gadhungal Research Group, result in much more than just the return of an object to the descendants of its makers. Community consultation opens entirely new avenues of research, which challenge deeply held beliefs about the ways museums have represented the Aboriginal and Torres Strait Island past. **MP**

'The sea carries the ship here, why'

In May 1770, *Endeavour* sailed along the Queensland coast off K'gari (Fraser Island). Watching its passage were the local Batjala people, who recorded the moment in oral history and song. Batjala linguist Gemma Cronin translated the below song and talks about its importance.

Gabrin wuna'la yaneen, Areeram
Ngun'gu'ni wiinj gung'milung
Nyundal wun'yamba dhali dhak'kin'bah,
Gebeer barine
Moomoo gumbir'l'im bundi buree, Yauwa
dhan man'ngur
Yuang yangu moomoo gumbir, Billi'ngunda
Tin'gera dan'da gung'mungalum minya?

Strangers are travelling with a cloud, Areeram!
It has fire inside, must be a bad water spirit.
It's stupid maybe? It's going directly to that rainbow serpent place,
This is the truth that I bring.
It is breathing smoke rhythmically from its rear, must be song men and sorcerers.
Coming up and going back with the wind at its rear, like a sand crab.
The sea carries the ship here, why?

This essay is an edited transcript of an interview with Gemma Cronin for the Australian National Maritime Museum's *Encounters* exhibition in 2020, which was cancelled due to the COVID-19 pandemic.

Indian Head by Peter **Hudson, 2013.** ANMM Collection 00054553

TO ME, that song is like a foretelling and a foreseeing, because even in the last line they say, 'The sea brought this ship here. Why? Why?'

So they're questioning what's happening. They're knowing that there's big changes coming. And you know what? That was the beginning of the end of a way of life for my people locally and Australia wide.

The descriptiveness of the ship, the way they described it was really in depth. So they said, first of all, 'Strangers are travelling with a cloud. He's got fire in his belly.' This is a cold time of year in my country and this must be a reference to people living inside the ship, the fires within for cooking and heating.

The song was sung when Captain Cook went past our island and travelled up the beach and our people saw it. Although I believe it was different to other ships they'd seen before, I don't believe it was the first time a ship that people lived upon had been seen, because of the word gung'-mungalum (water camp). That's an example of a language shift, a thing that happens linguistically when old cultures such as ours discover something new. They followed it from the bottom end of my island about two thirds of the way up. It was coming towards us and then going and then coming and going from side to side, like a sand crab.

I'm sure that mobs all along the east coast sang songs about this. It wouldn't have just been us. But what's different about us is that Cook was on the ship recording us singing and dancing at Corroboree Beach, just beside Tukki Wurru, which Cook named Indian Head.

As he could see our people standing up there, we were trying to warn him away from a dangerous shoal. He thought we were waving at him, and I think he called us Indians because we wear feathers culturally, us mob. I think that might've reminded him of the American Indians. He just called it Indian Head, straight up.

Tukki Wurru's a very important place to my people. It's part of our creation story of how this island was formed. It's focal in that story. And then it's where we had first contact, when everything changed, when colonialism was coming to our land, that is instrumental and focal in that as well. And then it's one of our first, not the only, but one of our first major and biggest massacre sites on the island.

So there's three really monumental things to me, as a Batjala woman, that that place has been a part of. I'm waiting to see what happens next. **GC**

TOP 'Minya?' ('Why?')

CENTRE 'Ngun'gu'ni wiinj.' ('Carrying the fire spirit within.')

ABOVE 'Nyin'nah.' ('I see.')

Stills from a video in which Gemma Cronin talks about the Batjala song that describes *Endeavour*'s arrival off the coast of K'gari (Fraser Island). Gemma Cronin is the cultural custodian and copyright owner of the song reproduced here.

Building the replica

The idea of a replica of *Endeavour*, as a tangible link with Australia's European heritage and James Cook, was conceived by maritime historian Bruce Stannard, then a member of the Australian National Maritime Museum's council. With council backing, he sought support from the corporate world and convinced Bond Corporation to take on the project in 1987.

The launch of the replica in 1993 was the culmination of the efforts of many people, and testament to their immensely specialised skills and knowledge.

Construction of a shipyard began in Fremantle, Western Australia, where the ship was to be assembled. There was also a rigging/sailmaking facility, blacksmith shop, drawing office and administration offices. To involve visitors and school groups, a viewing gallery, classrooms and a conference room were also included. More than 600,000 people visited while the vessel was being constructed.

To meet the museum's requirement for an exact and historically authentic replica of HM Bark *Endeavour*, original data had to be found. This was located at the National Maritime Museum, UK, and made available for the project. Among the key items were copies of the ship's draughts (plans). All of these drawings, done at different times, provided an amazing insight into the ship's conversion from a humble collier, *Earl of Pembroke*, to the fabulous 'as fitted' drawing, done on 11 July 1768 at Deptford, just before its historic first voyage. This small but wonderfully comprehensive plan revealed the long-gone glorious language of the 18th-century shipwright and his craft.

The construction process started with converting HM Bark *Endeavour*'s original ship's draughts to detailed working drawings. For the 20th-century shipwrights who had to plan the building of the replica, other fascinating sources of information were Cook's log and journals, the journals of Joseph Banks and the wonderful sketches made by Sydney Parkinson.

The timber used in the original vessel was a mixture of English oak and pine. As the replica vessel was to be built and used in the waters of the Antipodes, it was decided to use Australian hardwood. The principal wood used for the hull below the waterline, the wales and all the major structural components throughout the ship was Western Australian jarrah, with some tallowwood from New South Wales incorporated in the forward upper deck. To conserve natural resources, some of the ship's large components were laminated, while others were constructed from recycled timbers, such as old railway bridges. Other timbers used included douglas fir (oregon) and Western Australian karri.

The 20th-century fit-out was designed by naval architect Ken McAlpine. With sound engineering, lateral thinking and a complete understanding of the subject matter, Ken resolved the conflicting requirements of replicating a full-sized 18th-century sailing ship while meeting the demands of 20th- and 21st-century naval architecture, marine engineering, stability, habitability and safety requirements. The ship was built to USL 2A Classification, meeting the requirements for a wooden, twin-screw auxiliary, full-rigged sailing ship. This made it an insurable sailing ship: a vessel that was able to sail the oceans of the world on its own, just like its predecessor.

The launch of the *Endeavour* replica in Fremantle on 9 December 1993 was the culmination of the efforts of many people, and testament to their immensely specialised skills and knowledge. Since then, the ship has sailed twice around the globe, made more than 330 individual voyages, spent 1,900 days (5.2 years) sailing and carried approximately 14,500 passengers and crew in the footsteps of James Cook, Joseph Banks and their contemporaries. **BL**

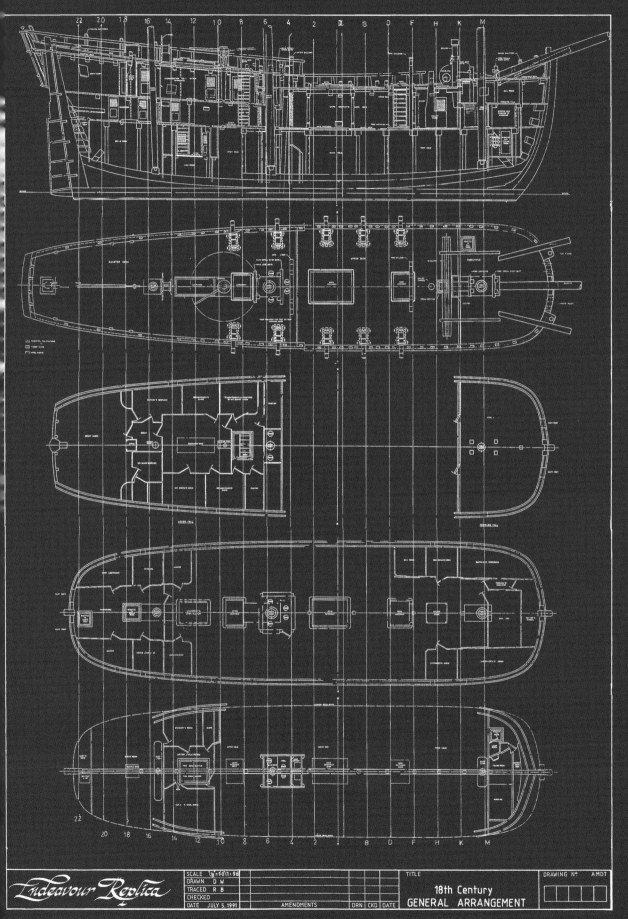

General arrangement of the *Endeavour* replica, 1991. ANMM Collection

A mighty endeavour

The *Endeavour* replica was built by literally hundreds of workers — young people who completed their apprenticeships on the project, volunteer guides who stayed with the ship throughout all the dramas of the build and beyond, extraordinarily skilled artisans and the initial crew who helped work out how the ship could operate in a different century. Decades after its launch, the ship continues to fascinate those who sail on and visit it.

RIGHT Shipwrights Carl Ollivierre and Danny McDermitt harvesting jarrah knees, January 1992.

When the build team found out that old spotted gums were being removed due to the widening of the Pacific Highway at Heron's Creek, NSW, they gained permission to harvest some of them for the ship's knees. These were cut in one piece from the junction of a tree's trunk and either a branch or a root. As the grain follows the natural curve of the tree, these 'grown' knees have greater strength than knees cut from the straight grain of sawn timber.

ABOVE Nev Casey cutting knees from a root.

RIGHT Les Oxenbridge with some of the hanging knees, which support the upper deck, after installation in the replica.

MAIN IMAGE The lower deck (looking forward) being caulked.

ABOVE The keel-laying ceremony, 22 October 1988. Western Australian Governor, Professor Gordon Reid, hammers a bolt into the fitting that holds the keel–stem scarph in place.

BELOW Blacksmith Jan Jensen in the traditional blacksmith shop that was constructed on the *Endeavour* build site.

FAR LEFT (top) Port side from aft showing floors and midship frames in place.

FAR LEFT (bottom) Fitting the shutter plank — the last plank below the waterline.

LEFT Sailmaker and rigger Glen Hope, and planking of the hull in progress.

ABOVE Fitting the wheel.

RIGHT The ship was painted in traditional colours of the time: red from vermillion, yellow from yellow ochre and blue from Prussian blue. Paints were made from original materials and methods and their colours then scanned and replicated in modern paints. Below the waterline, the ship was painted in white antifouling – on Cook's ship, a mixture of tallow and white lead was used.

LEFT *Endeavour* at a temporary berth in Fremantle Harbour, just after its launch on 9 December 1993. It then took another four months for it to be rigged. A jig had been built out in the courtyard of the build shed so that all the rigging could be assembled and tested prior to launch.

RIGHT *Endeavour* on its first day at sea with all sails set. The only problems found on that day were 20th-century ones, with the exhaust system and prop shafts. The 18th-century equipment all worked perfectly, vindicating one of the build team's key policies – not to out-think the original design, but simply to build it as it was.

LEFT The elaborate hull decorations were carved by celebrated Danish sculptor Jenny Scrayen to designs drawn by marine artist Ross Shardlow. The quarter window decoration on the Great Cabin was well documented on the drafts of *Endeavour* sourced from the National Maritime Museum, Greenwich. The stern was a bit of a mystery, though, with only a quick sketch by HMB *Endeavour* artist Sydney Parkinson to guide Ross Shardlow.

Images on pages 34–36 are by John Lancaster, Les Oxenbridge and unidentified photographers.

Endeavour replica facts and figures

Constructed
Fremantle, Western Australia

Keel laid
October 1988

Launched
9 December 1993

Commissioned
16 April 1994

Construction cost
$17 million + countless volunteer hours

Time to build
5 years

Rig type
Three-masted full-rigged ship

Sail
28 sails; sail area of 1,040 m² (10,000 sq feet)

Length
Overall length 32.75 m (length between perpendiculars 28.07 m)

Beam
9 metres

Draft
4 metres

Air draft
(height from waterline to top of mast)
36 metres

Gross tonnage
397 tonnes

Displacement
620 tonnes fully laden

Main engines
2 x Caterpillar 300 kW

Fuel capacity
36,000 litres (diesel)

Speed
Max 7 knots (13 km/h) under power; 11 knots (20 km/h) under sail

Crew and passengers
Day sails: 10 professional crew, 70 passengers
Offshore voyages: 16 professional crew, 36 amateur voyage crew, 4 supernumeraries (passengers)

Generators
2
(for electricity)

Fresh water capacity
12.384 tonnes

Fresh water production
3 tonnes per day (via a desalinator)

Sewage treatment plant
1

Sewage capacity
2.196 tonnes

Heads (toilets)
7

Showers
7

Voyages around the globe
2

Individual voyages made
More than 330

Passengers carried
More than 14,500

Days spent at sea
1,900 (5.2 years)

Key objects on the ship

When not sailing, the *Endeavour* replica is a floating museum. Props like these replicate the original objects as closely as possible and help to evoke life on board in the 18th century.

Sailor's palm

A leather tool that wraps around the hand. It is used to push sail needles through thick canvas or rope.

Ship's sextant

Navigational tool used to determine a ship's latitude by measuring the angular distance between the horizon and the sun.

Serving mallet

'Serving' is a small rope that is bound tightly around a larger rope to protect it. The serving mallet was used to apply these bindings.

Seat of ease

The ship's toilet. *Endeavour* had two, one at each side of the bow. This is why a ship's toilet is called a head — because it was at the head of the ship. The seat of ease was simply a barrel with an open bottom that was flushed by the waves. Instead of toilet paper, there was a 'rinsing rope' with an unravelled end, as pictured. This trailed permanently in the sea and was pulled up when needed.

Log line and timer

Used together to measure a ship's speed. The log line is knotted at intervals of 48 feet (approximately 14.6 metres). It is dropped into the water and the timer started, and the crew then measures how many 'knots' of line reel out in 30 seconds. This is the origin of the term 'knots', meaning nautical miles per hour.

Trunnel

Both HMB *Endeavour* and the replica were fastened with wooden pegs known as trunnels, or 'tree nails'. HMB *Endeavour* used only trunnels, as they do not corrode like metal nails. This trunnel was sent aboard the space shuttle *Endeavour* on its maiden voyage in 1992, before being hammered into the stern post in the replica's Great Cabin. It is identified by a bronze ring.

Cannon (replica)

HMB *Endeavour* carried 10 four-pounder cannons. Six of these were jettisoned to lighten the ship after it ran aground on **Endeavour** Reef, Queensland, in 1770. The replica has four cannons, which were manufactured in Australia.

All images ANMM

HMB *Endeavour* in America

The final role of HMB *Endeavour*'s career was as a sacrificial bit-player in the American Revolutionary War. Its scuttled remains then lay forgotten in the mud of Newport Harbor, Rhode Island, for more than two centuries.

THE AMERICAN Revolutionary War began in 1775, when armed clashes between British troops and the Massachusetts militia escalated into a general uprising that saw British troops besieged in Boston. For the preceding decade or more, there had been growing unrest in Britain's American colonies over lack of parliamentary representation and the imposition of taxes, but the uprising in Boston raised the stakes considerably.

Britain's immediate response was to reinforce its troops in New York and Boston, with further plans to send 27,000 infantry — a scheme that required contracting hundreds of private ships to transport the soldiers across the Atlantic. Cook's *Endeavour* (now renamed *Lord Sandwich* and in private hands) became one of these transports and sailed with a large fleet that arrived off New York in August 1776.

In December the ship was on the move again, this time as part of a fleet carrying 7,000 troops to control the strategically important town of Newport, Rhode Island, midway between New York and Boston. The British grip on the area was far from secure, and *Lord Sandwich* and other vessels were used to lock up the town's revolutionary sympathisers whenever necessary.

The situation deteriorated dramatically after the surrender of a British army of 6,000 men to Revolutionary forces at Saratoga, New York, in October 1777 — a success that finally resolved France to send a naval squadron to challenge the British position in New England.

When, in July 1778, the French squadron suddenly arrived off Rhode Island threatening to overwhelm the town and to capture the small British naval force stationed there, the senior British officer in charge ordered the burning of nine Royal Navy vessels and the sinking of many transports in the shipping channels around Newport to impede the French from bombarding the town. *Lord Sandwich* was one of them.

A note from the agent in charge of transports explains why *Lord Sandwich* and other older transports were left under water:

Those ships sunk off the different batteries [gun emplacements] in the channels cannot possibly be weighed [raised] from the depth of water and a very heavy gale of wind coming on a few days after they were sunk and the age of the vessels, most of them being very weak.

When the French took control of Newport in 1779, *Lord Sandwich* and the other vessels, sunk the previous year, were left to gradually disappear under the mud in Newport's outer harbour. **NE**

French archival map from 1778, showing location of scuttled transports (including *Lord Sandwich/Endeavour*) between Goat Island and Newport's North Battery (indicated within faint dotted line).
Norman B Leventhal Map & Education Centre, Boston Public Library

A very long search

Tantalising clues that the remains of HMB *Endeavour* might lie in Newport Harbor emerged in the late 1990s. Fieldwork and archival research over the next two decades led to the ship's eventual identification in 2022.

THE SEARCH for Cook's *Endeavour* has its origins in the birth of maritime archaeology. Derived from Greek, the term 'archaeology' literally means 'the study of ancient history', but more generally it is understood as the study of human activity through the recovery and analysis of material culture — the stuff those humans left behind. Archaeology really took off in the late 19th and early 20th centuries, with the excavation of ancient sites around the Mediterranean Sea, but until a convenient means of working under water was invented, it remained almost entirely a land-based activity.

The breakthrough came with the invention of the aqualung — also known as 'self-contained underwater breathing apparatus', or scuba — in 1946. Before then, divers used hard-hat suits and were restricted in their mobility by ropes and air hoses connected to the surface. The aqualung opened the underwater world to recreational divers and soon led to some surprising discoveries.

In the 1960s and 70s, the remains of four Dutch East India Company ships — *Batavia* (1629), *Vergulde Draeck* (1656), *Zuytdorp* (1712) and *Zeewijk* (1727) — were located in Western Australia. More discoveries soon followed: the wrecks of HMS *Pandora*, lost on the Great Barrier Reef in 1791, and the flagship of the First Fleet, HMS *Sirius*, wrecked at Norfolk Island a year earlier. While in most cases much of the structure of these ships had disappeared, divers

Multibeam Echo Sounder image of the seabed in Newport Harbor, showing the wreck sites of British transports scuttled in 1778. Within the dotted line lie several sites, one of which, designated RI 2394, was identified as the remains of *Endeavour* in 2022. Image United States National Oceanographic and Atmospheric Administration (NOAA)

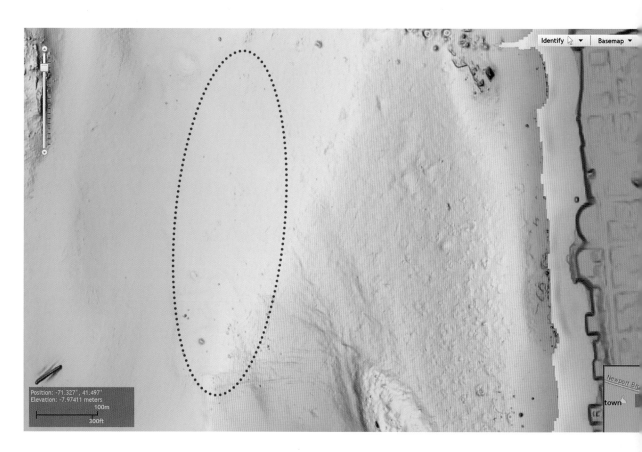

Position: -71.327°, 41.497°
Elevation: -7.97411 meters
100m
300ft

were surprised by the range of objects that survived — from sturdy anchors and cannons to fragile objects, such as leather shoes, rope, ceramic tableware and glass bottles. The realisation that shipwrecks and other underwater sites potentially contained rich material culture led to both a need for legal protection of sites and the establishment of specialised conservation laboratories to treat material recovered from under water.

In the USA, the *Abandoned Shipwrecks Act* passed by the federal government in 1988 sought to protect historic shipwrecks by transferring responsibility to the states in whose waters the wrecks lay. In Rhode Island the state government assumed legal title for certain wrecks and appointed a commission to administer its responsibilities in relation to them. The legal framework recognised the potential historical importance of shipwrecks, but until the creation of the Rhode Island Marine Archaeology Project (RIMAP) in 1992, relatively little underwater investigation had taken place. Local historians knew of the transports sunk in Newport in 1778, but once researchers in 1998 established that Cook's ship HMB *Endeavour* had been one of these, investigating the transports became a major focus of RIMAP activities. A year later the Australian National Maritime Museum started a collaboration with RIMAP that resulted in maritime archaeologists and conservators from the museum regularly participating in fieldwork in Rhode Island over the next 20 years.

The painstaking investigation, both under water and in historical archives, finally led to HMB *Endeavour*'s identification in 2022. **NE**

Why search for shipwrecks?

In other parts of this book you can read about the recovery of *Endeavour* relics thrown overboard at Endeavour Reef and the long search to identify *Endeavour*'s final resting place in the United States, which raises the question — why do we feel compelled to undertake such actions?

At one level it can be simply part of an anniversary celebration, as in the case of the 1969 Endeavour Reef expedition (in the lead-up to the Cook bicentenary) and the 1987 *Sirius* expedition at Norfolk Island (for the 1988 bicentenary of European settlement in Australia). Every country has its own personalities and events that loom large in its national psyche and that, at their best, help create a sense of national cohesion and identity.

At other times we may simply feel compelled out of a sense of respect and the need to provide closure — as was the motivation in the search for the Australian cruiser HMAS *Sydney* (II) and its crew of over 600 men that were lost in 1941, and the search for the Australian submarine *AE1* that disappeared in 1914 off Rabaul in Papua New Guinea.

Newspaper photograph of officers and crew from submarine *AE1* and its sister ship *AE2*, 1914. ANMM Collection Gift from Jennifer Smyth

There is, however, also a more compelling fascination with some objects, based on how they can link us directly to a time and place beyond our own. The objects (then known as 'curiosities') that Joseph Banks and others brought back to England aboard the *Endeavour* caused a sensation in London, providing the first glimpses into the cultures of the Pacific. Archaeologist Mary Beaudry has described this as a process of 'communicating about the unknown by means of the known'. It is precisely that ability that continues to provide a powerful motivation for archaeology and the investigation of our past. **NE**

Diving on the wreck

Diving on the *Endeavour* wreck takes skill, concentration — and the right kit. Maritime archaeologist Dr James Hunter models the typical outfit for a dive on the wreck, which sits in 12 metres of murky and often cold water in Newport Harbor, Rhode Island.

'Primary' regulator
Enables diver to breathe the air in the scuba cylinder.

'Secondary' regulator
(or 'octopus') Serves as a backup to the primary regulator. Can also be used by another diver for 'buddy-breathing' in an emergency if they run out of air.

Drysuit inflator
Is connected to the scuba cylinder and allows the diver to add air to their drysuit. A layer of air prevents the drysuit from squeezing the diver and also helps keeps them warm.

Lead weights
These counteract the buoyancy created by air in the diver's drysuit and BCD.

Padding at knees
Enables the diver to kneel on the seabed without risking tears or holes in the drysuit fabric.

Fins
Propel the diver through the water quickly and efficiently.

Images Jasmine Poole/ANMM

Auto-inflator for Buoyancy Compensation Device (BCD)
This device enables diver to control their descent and ascent and to maintain neutral buoyancy.

Safety whistle
To attract attention above the water.

Dump valve
Allows diver to remove excess air from the drysuit. Can be used in conjunction with the BCD to neutralise buoyancy.

Folding ruler
Can be used to take measurements on small objects, such as individual timbers and artefacts.

Underwater digital camera
Used to take both still photographs and video. This camera includes adjustable lights, a tray with handles and a clip to attach it to the diver's BCD.

Dive computer
Provides critical information, including depth, dive duration and time remaining before the diver needs to return to the surface.

Stainless steel clips
Enable diver to attach equipment and gauges to the BCD. This clip holds the diver's air gauge, which monitors the amount of air remaining in the cylinder.

'Pee-valve'
Enables diver to urinate under water if the need arises.

Knife
Can be used by a diver to cut free from entanglements (such as fishing line or rope). Most divers wear at least two knives in different locations so one is always accessible.

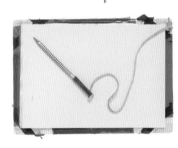

Photo scale
Divided into equal increments (here, 10 centimetres), and placed next to an artefact or hull feature when it is being photographed.

Plastic slate
For recording information while under water. Sheets of Mylar plastic film are attached to the slate and can be written or drawn on with pencil. The pencil has a lanyard so it doesn't float away.

Reel tapes
Used to measure large artefacts and hull features, and for taking measurements over long distances. They can also be used as a fixed 'baseline' that serves as a reference point from which other measurements are collected.

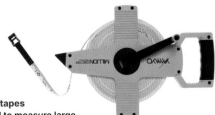

Working in the murk

People have preconceived notions about diving on shipwrecks – usually, that they're always in warm, tropical waters and surrounded by lots of fish.

Diving in Newport Harbor is nothing like that. The water is murky, turbid and greenish brown. There's 1 or 1.5 metres of visibility if you're lucky; some days, you can't see your hand in front of your face. Spotting a single fish is a rare treat.

The water temperature varies from cold in summer to *really* cold in winter. During site investigations in January 2020, the water temperature hovered just above freezing, but the air temperature was closer to minus 12 degrees C. When we entered the water, we suffered instant 'ice-cream headaches'. By the end of our dives, our hands and the exposed parts of our faces were completely numb from the cold.

Endeavour's shipwreck site is relatively featureless. The ends of eroded timbers barely protrude from the seabed in a faint line, and a few cannons are visible, but the rest of the site is buried in muddy silt. Because of this, it's very easy to get lost, which can be unnerving. When some of the structure of the wreck is uncovered, though, it becomes easier to find your way around. The more of the site we exposed and examined, the more we realised we were dealing with the remains of *Endeavour*.

We feel very fortunate to have interacted with and identified the shipwreck of this world-famous vessel.

Kieran Hosty and
James Hunter

Gathering the evidence

Positive identification of *Endeavour*'s shipwreck site was the culmination of several lines of evidence, but it was four specific 'Eureka' moments that enabled the museum's maritime archaeology team to solve the puzzle.

1.
Connecting the transport *Lord Sandwich* and HMB *Endeavour*

AS EARLY as 1828, Newport, Rhode Island, was identified as the place where *Endeavour* ended its days, having reportedly been abandoned there after a lengthy post-Royal Navy career as a French-owned whaling ship named *La Liberté*. However, research conducted in the 1990s by Australian historians Mike Connell and Des Liddy revealed that *La Liberté* was in fact another of James Cook's vessels of exploration, HMS *Resolution*. Connell and Liddy also found an entry in the 1778 edition of *Lloyd's Register of Shipping* that listed a ship named *Lord Sandwich* that shared many of HMB *Endeavour*'s characteristics, including its tonnage and place of construction. Intriguingly, its former name was also listed as 'Endeavour'. The link between *Lord Sandwich* and HMB *Endeavour* was confirmed in 1999 by Dr Kathy Abbass, who discovered additional historical information that revealed the two ships were one and the same, and that *Lord Sandwich* was one of several British transports intentionally sunk in Newport Harbor in 1778 during the American Revolutionary War.

2.
Discovery of the 'Knowles Document'

In 2015, the museum's former Head of Research, Dr Nigel Erskine, conducted archival research at the British Public Records Office (now UK National Archives) in London. There he discovered historical documents that would prove critical in the effort to identify *Endeavour*'s wreck site. One was a letter written by Lieutenant John Knowles, a British Army officer who oversaw the fleet of transport ships in Newport Harbor in 1778 and ordered several of them scuttled as blockships in the lead-up to the Battle of Rhode Island. In the letter, Knowles identified general geographic areas within the harbour where specific transports were sunk. One of these zones, located within waters between the northern end of Goat Island and Newport's historic North Battery, was identified as the location where *Lord Sandwich* (formerly HMB *Endeavour*) was scuttled in August 1778. Four other vessels were also sunk in this area, and of the group, *Lord Sandwich* was clearly the largest, with a carrying capacity more than 100 tons greater than the next-biggest ship. Erskine's discovery

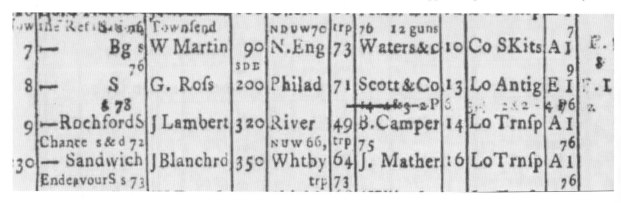

ABOVE Entry in *Lloyd's Register of Shipping* from 1778 showing the tonnage and place of construction of *Lord Sandwich*, and that its former name was *Endeavour*. Lloyd's Register Foundation Heritage & Education Centre

Copy of Letter from Lieutenant
John Knowles Agent for Transports
at Newport Rhode Island dated
12 Sept 1778 to the Navy Board

In consequence of an order from
Captain Brisbane Senior Officer of his Majesty's
Ships &c at Newport (a Copy of which I enclose),
the undermentioned Transports & Victualing
Vessels were scuttled and sunk, the Stores &c
which were saved belonging to them, will, as
soon as collected be delivered to the Commanding
Officer to be disposed of for the Benefit of the
Crown I am. &c

Sunk between Goat Island
and Rose Island ———
Good Intent ———
Rachel & Mary ———
Susannah
Union

Between the Blue Rocks and
Pest Island
Bristol
Malaga
Esther

Between Goat Island
and the North Battery
Lord Sandwich
Earl of Orford
Yowart
Peggy
May Flower

Between the Lime
Rocks & Goat
Island in the
S° Channell
Lucy

of this document reduced the total number
of shipwreck candidates from 13 to five, and
narrowed the search area from nearly 10 square
kilometres to only 0.25 square kilometres.

ABOVE Letter by John Knowles
identifying where in Newport
Harbor specific transports were
sunk. Image Nigel Erskine

BELOW Remnants of RI 2394's
bilge pump assembly and well.
Images James Hunter

3.
Identification of RI 2394's surviving bilge pump assembly and well

Following Erskine's discovery in 2015,
research in Newport Harbor focused on the
area, specified in the Knowles Document,
where *Lord Sandwich* was reportedly scuttled.
Ultimately, four 18th-century shipwreck sites
were discovered in waters between the north
end of Goat Island and the North Battery.
The largest of these shipwrecks — given the
Rhode Island archaeological site number
RI 2394 — became the focus of study in 2018.
One of the earliest indicators that it might be
Endeavour was the size of the shipwreck's
visible timbers. It was clear from the outset
that RI 2394 represented the remnants of
a relatively large, wooden-hulled sailing
vessel, and measurements of its individual
timbers closely matched historical records
of HMB *Endeavour's* construction.

Another significant line of evidence
connecting RI 2394 and *Endeavour* are the
types of timber species used to construct
the hull. Timber sampling of RI 2394's hull
components in 2018, 2019 and 2021 revealed
the majority were hewn from white oak. The
lone exception was the vessel's keel in the
midships area, which was manufactured from
elm. The exclusive use of white oak and elm
in the shipwreck's construction is indicative
of a vessel built in a British shipyard — North
American shipbuilders used a much wider
selection of timbers and did not use elm

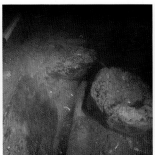
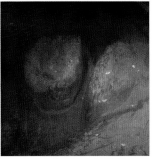

The survival of the keel–stem scarph — a highly diagnostic feature — was critical to the identification of the wreck site as HMB *Endeavour*

for their keel. It also exactly matches information about HMB *Endeavour*'s construction in an Admiralty survey from 1768, which specifies that its framing and keel were hewn from English oak and elm, respectively.

One of the most critical leaps forward in identifying the wreck came in 2019, when remnants of its bilge pump assembly and well were identified. All ships leaked, and consequently were fitted with bilge pumps to ensure seawater that entered the hull could be removed so the vessel remained afloat. Bilge pumps fitted to 18th-century English ships typically comprised a minimum of two hollow wooden shafts that extended from the lowest part of the hull (bilge) to the upper (weather) deck. Most vessels also featured a pump well that housed the lower sections of the bilge pumps.

Discovery of the surviving pump assembly and well was a significant turning point in the identification of the site. It was a recognisable structural feature that allowed the museum's maritime archaeologists, Kieran Hosty and Dr James Hunter, to positively identify the wreck's midships section. It could also be compared with the pump well included on archival plans of *Endeavour*. When RI 2394's site plan was superimposed over *Endeavour*'s 1768 lower hold plan and scaled to the same size, the positions of the surviving pump shaft stump and pump well partitions aligned perfectly with their counterparts on the archival document. Superimposition of the site plan and 1768 ship plans also allowed Hosty and Hunter to predict the location of the bow end of the shipwreck's keel, which was confirmed during subsequent investigations of the site in 2021.

4.
The keel–stem scarph

Discovery of the bow revealed a distinctive scarph, or join, in the surviving keel timber that attached it to the vessel's stempost (which is no longer there). The survival of the keel–stem scarph — a highly diagnostic feature — was critical to the identification of the wreck site as *Endeavour*. It permitted the project team to obtain a measurement from the stem (bow) end of the keel to the projected location of the mainmast, which almost exactly matched the same distance shown on archival plans of *Endeavour*. There is a slight variation of roughly 20 centimetres between the two

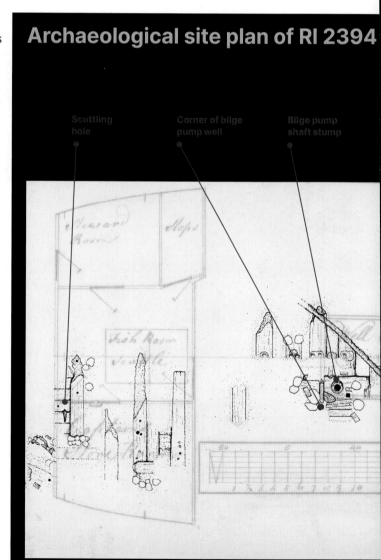

Archaeological site plan of RI 2394

Scuttling hole

Corner of bilge pump well

Bilge pump shaft stump

measurements — probably the result of damage to the end of the keel caused by natural degradation.

Documentation of the scarph also provided critical details about its design and construction. RI 2394's example is a rare form of stem attachment known as a 'half-lap' scarph. It allowed the stem to have a near-vertical rake, necessary for a vessel requiring the broad, bluff bow typical of a Whitby collier. RI 2394's keel–stem scarph was significantly different from the 'table' and 'box' scarphs typically used in mid-to-late-18th-century British shipbuilding. When compared with the keel–stem scarph shown on *Endeavour*'s 1768 Admiralty plan, it was an exact match in terms of form and size.

Furthermore, a survey of extant mid-to-late-18th-century ship plans held in the collections of the National Maritime Museum in Greenwich, UK, revealed construction details for 40 individual vessels, only one of which displayed a keel–stem scarph like that observed on RI 2394. That vessel, *Marquis of Rockingham*, was another Whitby collier built by Thomas Fishburn — the owner and master shipwright of the shipyard where *Endeavour* was constructed. *Marquis of Rockingham* was later commissioned by the Royal Navy and renamed HMS *Raleigh,* but is perhaps best known as one of James Cook's other vessels of exploration, HMS *Adventure.* KH, JH

Archaeological site plan of RI 2394, by James Hunter. Superimposed over a plan from 1768 of *Endeavour*'s lower hold, from Royal Museums Greenwich.

The archaeological site map of RI 2394, when superimposed over a 1768 plan of *Endeavour* 's lower hold, showed measurements and other significant features that matched almost perfectly.

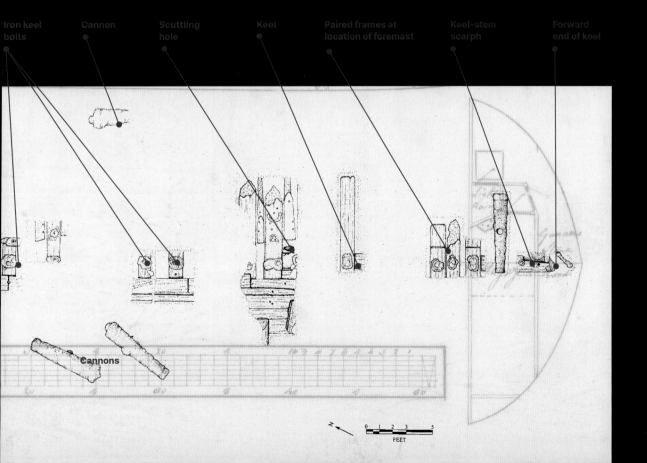

Iron keel bolts

Cannon

Scuttling hole

Keel

Paired frames at location of foremast

Keel–stem scarph

Forward end of keel

Cannons

FEET

What's next for Cook's *Endeavour*?

FOR THE first few years after being scuttled, *Endeavour* would have remained largely intact. But over two centuries, the masts and rigging would have either been removed or collapsed to the seabed, while the timber hull would have gradually succumbed to the elements and human activity (such as anchor drags, laying of cables, and sweeping of the seabed for obstructions). Eventually, only the lowest part of the hull remained and was largely buried by successive layers of marine growth and silt.

What should happen now? It is highly unlikely the shipwreck will ever be recovered in its entirety for two reasons: one, there's probably not enough left of it to raise (only about 15 per cent of the lowermost hull survives) and secondly, the cost and time involved. A safe estimate is that it could cost as much as $US 250 million and take 30 years to complete archaeological analysis and conservation of the surviving hull and artefacts.

There's also the question: Why do it? *Endeavour* holds a particular and multi-layered place in the Australian story, but in the United States, the vessel — known as *Lord Sandwich* at the time it was scuttled — was just one of several troop transports and prison ships in operation during the American Revolutionary War. So far, the shipwreck has yielded very few artefacts, though much of the site remains to be explored.

In coming years, there is plenty to do to secure the wreck site and protect what is left for future exploration and interpretation — and to tell *Endeavour*'s story for future generations. At a minimum, this should include additional survey work to locate and confirm the northern (stern) extremity of the surviving hull remains, as well as assess the condition of the site's four iron cannons. Efforts should also be made to replace each cannon's existing protective anodes and install additional anodes for their ongoing preservation, if necessary.

Further excavation should also be undertaken to locate and document evidence of *Endeavour*'s other bilge pumps, as well as assess the archaeological potential of sediment deposits on the starboard side of the hull, which is more deeply buried and probably better preserved. As new hull features are uncovered, they can be recorded and added to the existing site plan. This in turn will provide a better understanding of *Endeavour*'s framing and lower hull architecture. The timber 'skeleton' that formed the foundation of the ship's construction is not well documented in historical sources, nor are specifics of changes made to it over time — such as repairs carried out in the wake of the grounding on Endeavour Reef. Ultimately, it is archaeology that will fill these gaps in our understanding and help paint a more complete picture of *Endeavour*'s lengthy and varied history. **KH, JH**

Irini Malliaros (left) and Kieran Hosty excavate the *Endeavour* shipwreck site in September 2019. Image James Hunter

About the authors

Gemma Cronin is a Batjala linguist, songwoman and poet. Her ongoing research into *Endeavour*'s appearance off K'gari (Fraser Island) has inspired significant artistic and cultural projects representing the historical and contemporary lives of Batjala people.

Dr Nigel Erskine is a maritime archaeologist and retired Head of Research at the Australian National Maritime Museum. He participated in the search for the remains of HMB *Endeavour* in Newport, Rhode Island, over several field seasons and his archival research was instrumental in identifying the location of the vessel.

Nick Flood is never more at home than when his hands are dirty, and as Senior Conservator — Special Projects at the Australian National Maritime Museum, he is frequently up to his elbows. Nick has conservation expertise in metals, functional objects, maritime archaeology and photographic documentation.

Jeffrey Fox has over 10 years' experience working across private and institutional sectors in Australia and internationally. Jeff is Senior Conservator — Collections at the Australian National Maritime Museum. He enjoys planning and leading conservation activities related to the museum's collection, preventive conservation and arranging outgoing loans.

Dr Peter Hobbins is a historian of science, technology and medicine. He has published widely on maritime and aviation history, immigration and quarantine, pandemics and medical science. Peter is Head of Content at the Australian National Maritime Museum, where he leads the exhibitions, curatorial, library and publishing teams.

Kieran Hosty is Maritime Archaeology Manager at the Australian National Maritime Museum, where he also curates the museum's collection relating to convicts, 19th-century migrants and ship technology. He has worked on many maritime archaeological projects both in Australia and overseas, including the hunt for Cook's *Endeavour* in the USA.

Dr James Hunter is Curator of Naval Heritage and Archaeology at the Australian National Maritime Museum. He has been involved in the fields of historical and maritime archaeology for over two decades and participated in the investigation of several internationally significant shipwreck sites, including that of HMB *Endeavour* in the USA.

Bill Leonard AM underwent a traditional shipbuilding apprenticeship in Scotland before moving to Western Australia in 1987. He was a master shipwright in the construction of the replicas of HMB *Endeavour* and of *Duyfken*, the VOC (Dutch East India Company) ship that was the first European vessel to visit and chart part of Australia.

Anthony Longhurst is the Master of the *Endeavour* replica. From 1995 until 2000 he sailed with *Endeavour* as a watch leader, shipwright, sailmaker and boatswain on its first world voyage. Anthony rejoined *Endeavour* in 2005 when it came under the management of the Australian National Maritime Museum.

John Longley sailed in five consecutive America's Cup campaigns, including on *Australia II* during its historic win in 1983. He managed the *Endeavour* replica project from its inception until 1999 and is a former chairman of the foundation that initially owned and operated the *Duyfken* replica.

Prof John Maynard is a Worimi man from the Port Stephens region of New South Wales. He is a historian whose publications have focused on the intersections of Aboriginal political and social history, and the history of Australian race relations.

Matt Poll is a Torres Strait Island and Loyalty Island curator of the Watego family and the manager of Indigenous programs at the Australian National Maritime Museum. Matt previously worked as Curator of Indigenous Heritage Collections and Repatriation Project Officer of the Macleay Museum and Chau Chak Wing Museum at the University of Sydney.

Index

Acknowledgments

For their assistance in producing this book, the museum wishes to thank all of the authors, as well as Sharon Babbage, Susan Davidson, Sally Fletcher, Linda Hardy, Ally Hyde, Judy Kim, Jasmine Poole, Karen Pymble and the many volunteers who help our visitors to interpret the *Endeavour* replica.

OPPOSITE The *Endeavour* replica encounters a humpback whale off Bond Beach, NSW.
Image Isaac Poulsen